Beehives and Bumbleberries

DESIGNS BY

Ann Danzig

Brent Severe

Suzanne Severe

EAGLE
GATE

SALT LAKE CITY, UTAH

Every effort has been made to ensure that all instructions are accurate and complete. The authors and publisher cannot, however, be responsible for the finished product due to human error, techniques, material used, or variations in individual work.

Library of Congress Cataloging-in-Publication Data

Beehives and bumbleberries.
    p.   cm.
   ISBN 1-57008-786-5
    1. Textile crafts—Utah.   2. Arts, Mormon—Utah.
TT699 .B44 2002
746'.90792—dc21   2001006714

Printed in the United States of America
K.P. Corporation, Salt Lake City, UT   48068-6921

10   9   8   7   6   5   4   3   2   1

Contents

Beyond the Garden Gate Quilt

Approximate size: 60" x 42"

SUPPLIES

4 yards of green print fabric for background of garden gate appliqué, inside border, and piping or bias for binding (this is the center background fabric)

1 yard of yellow print fabric for outside border

¼ yard of green check fabric for background of three beehives appliqué

¼ yard of peach print fabric for background of hand appliqué

Fat quarter of blue print fabric for background of tall beehive appliqué

Fat quarter of peach print fabric for background of boot appliqué

Fat quarter of blue print fabric for background of watering can appliqué

Fat quarter of lavender print fabric for background of heart jar appliqué

⅝ yard of off-white print fabric for garden gate appliqué

Fat quarters or fabric scraps for appliqué pieces as follows:

 1 off-white solid or muslin piece for fence post trim and balls, border on watering can, and inside of heart jar

 7 coordinating gold prints for all beehives, center of flowers and berries, and 1 heart in jar

 3 contrasting purple prints or plaids for 2 flowers, all boot pieces, and 1 heart in jar

 2 coordinating mauve prints for flowers in boot, ribbon on beehives, spout and handle on watering can, and 1 heart in jar

 2 coordinating peach prints for 1 flower, contrasting spout piece on watering can, flowers for border on watering can, and heart jar cover

4 coordinating green prints for stems and leaves of flowers in boot, flower leaves, trim on border of watering can, and bow on heart jar

1 brown print for center of flowers in boot

1 tan print for hinges on gate

2 cranberry or burgundy prints for berries and 1 heart in jar

1 yellow print for watering can

1 blue stripe for border of heart jar

1 blue print (or scrap from tall beehive background) for 1 heart in jar

1 flesh solid fabric for hands

7 yards of ⅛" cording for binding

3 yards of fabric for backing

Three ½" burgundy buttons for center of flowers in watering can

Twelve ¼" black buttons for hinges of garden gate

15 bee-shaped clay buttons

CUTTING

Cut a 10¾" wide x 19" high block of fabric for background of tall beehive appliqué.

Cut a 10¾" wide x 9" high block of fabric for background of boot appliqué.

Cut two 2" x 10¾" strips of center background fabric for use as dividing pieces.

Cut four 2" x 6¼" strips of center background fabric for use as dividing pieces.

Cut a 23½" wide x 6¼" high block of fabric for background of three beehives appliqué.

Cut a 23½" wide x 6¼" high block of fabric for background of hands appliqué.

Cut a 26½" wide x 17½" high block of center background fabric for gate appliqué.

Cut a 10¾" wide x 9" high block of fabric for background of heart jar appliqué.

Cut a 10¾" wide x 19" high block of fabric for background of watering can appliqué.

Cut two 2" x 30" strips and two 2" x 50" strips of center background fabric for the inside border.

Cut two 5" x 32" strips and two 5" x 60" strips of the yellow print fabric used for the outside border. (You will need to piece the 60" long strips together.)

ASSEMBLY

Sew a 2" x 10¾" strip of center background fabric to the bottom edge of the fabric block for the tall beehive background. Sew the bottom edge of the center background strip to the top of the boot background fabric block, as shown in Figure A.

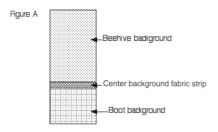

Figure A
— Beehive background
— Center background fabric strip
— Boot background

Sew a 2" x 6¼" strip of center background fabric to each short side of the three beehives background piece, as shown in Figure B. Sew a 2" x 6¼" strip of center background fabric to each short side of the hands background piece, also shown in Figure B.

Figure B   Three Beehives & Hands backgrounds

Attach the two strips created above (the hands appliqué background and the three beehives appliqué background) to the top and bottom of the center background fabric to be used for the gate appliqué, as shown in Figure C.

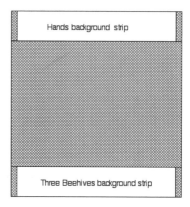

Figure C
Hands background strip
Three Beehives background strip

Sew a 2" x 10¾" strip of center background fabric to the bottom edge of the heart jar background fabric block, then sew the bottom edge of the center background strip to the top of the watering can background fabric block, as shown in Figure D.

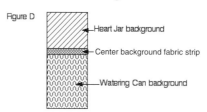

Figure D
— Heart Jar background
— Center background fabric strip
— Watering Can background

Sew block from Figure D to the left side of Figure C panel; then sew block from Figure A to the right side of Figure C panel, as shown in Figure E.

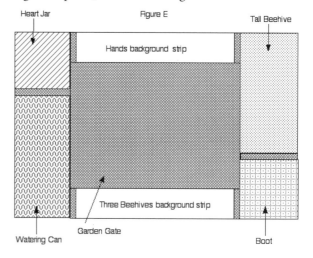

Heart Jar   Figure E   Tall Beehive
Hands background strip
Three Beehives background strip
Watering Can   Garden Gate   Boot

Following General Instructions, sew the 2" x 30" inside border strips to the sides of the panel from Figure E; trim as needed. Sew the 2" x 50" inside border strips to the top and bottom of the panel.

Sew the 5" x 32" outside border strips to sides of quilt top and trim as needed. Sew the 5" x 60" outside border strips to the top and bottom of quilt top and trim as needed.

Enlarge appliqué patterns as shown on the following pages. Quick-fuse or hand appliqué designs to background pieces as shown on sample. Many designs will overlap onto an adjoining background piece.

Trace a scalloped edge onto outside border. Start in each corner and work to the center. Adjust scallop to fit. Layer and quilt using your favorite method. Trim on traced scallop line through all thicknesses. Cover 1⁄8" cording with a 7 yard length of continuous 1" bias strip to create piping for the scalloped edge, or simply bind the quilt with a bias binding.

Embellish quilt with bee-shaped buttons sewn on the watering can, beehives, and flowers. Sew burgundy buttons to centers of flowers on watering can; sew 3 black buttons to each hinge on the garden gate.

First enlarge heart jar appliqué 200 percent, then enlarge 147 percent.

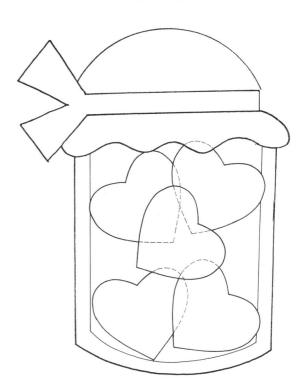

First enlarge watering can appliqué 200 percent, then enlarge 127 percent.

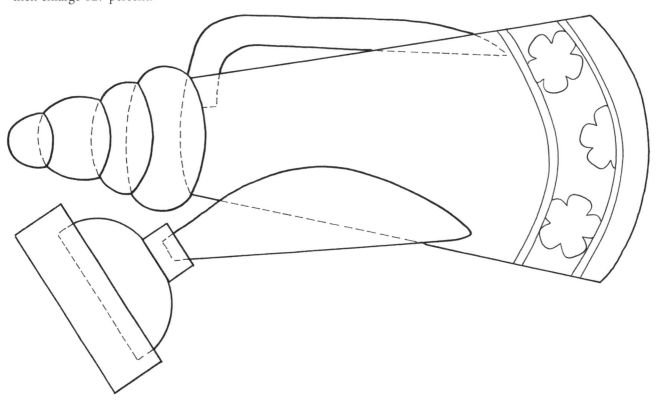

First enlarge the tall beehive and boot appliqués 200 percent, then enlarge 135 percent.

Enlarge hand and small beehive appliqués 200 percent.

"Bee Ye Humble" Wall Hanging

Approximate size: 15" x 21"

SUPPLIES

Fat quarters, 3 from pastel prints and 1 in muslin, for background blocks

Fat quarters or fabric scraps in assorted solids and prints for appliqué pieces:

> 5 gold solids for beehives
>
> 3 contrasting purple solids for boot, and the flowers on hat and wheelbarrow
>
> 2 coordinating mauve prints for flowers in boot
>
> 1 green print for leaves
>
> 1 burgundy print for berries
>
> 3 contrasting pastels for wheel
>
> 2 contrasting prints for dress, apron, and hat ties
>
> 1 tan or yellow print for hat
>
> 1 flesh solid for face, legs, and hand
>
> 1 brown solid for boots, wheelbarrow handle, and center of flowers in the boot

⅛ yard of contrasting print for inside border

¼ yard of contrasting print for outside border and binding

1 fat quarter of fabric for backing

DMC floss: #310 *Charcoal Black,* #221 *Bumbleberry Red,* #469 *Fir Green,* #801 *Dark Oak Brown,* #838 *Bark Brown*

Embroidery hoop and needle

3 bee-shaped clay buttons

Powder blush and cotton swab

CUTTING

Cut a 10¾" x 8¾" background block for girl appliqué.

Cut a 10¾" x 4¼" muslin block for embroidered verse.

Cut a 5¾" x 5¼" background block for boot appliqué.

Cut a 5½" x 5¼" background block for beehive appliqué.

Cut two 1" x 17¼" strips for sides and two 1" x 12" strips for top and bottom of inside border.

Cut two 2" x 18¼" strips for sides and two 2" x 15" strips for top and bottom of outside border.

Cut a 17" x 23" piece of fabric for backing.

ASSEMBLY

Enlarge patterns 130 percent.

Transfer lettering for embroidered verse to background block and backstitch words using 3 strands of DMC #469 *Fir Green* floss.

Sew boot and beehive background blocks together on one of the 5¼" sides, as shown in Figure A.

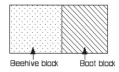

Figure A

Beehive block   Boot block

Sew background block for girl appliqué to top of embroidered verse block, as shown in Figure B.

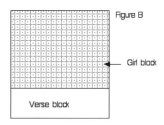

Figure B

Girl block

Verse block

Sew unit from Figure A to bottom of unit from Figure B, as shown in Figure C.

13

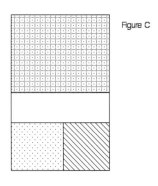

Figure C

Using your favorite appliqué method, fuse or handstitch appliqué designs to corresponding background blocks according to pattern illustration.

Embroider flower stems with a vine stitch using 3 strands of DMC #838 *Bark Brown* floss.

Backstitch lines for girl's shoelaces using 2 strands of DMC #310 *Charcoal Black* floss; make French knots for eyes with same thread.

Backstitch lines for hair using 2 strands of DMC #801 *Dark Oak Brown* floss.

Backstitch vines in hat using 1 strand DMC #801 *Dark Oak Brown* floss.

Make French knots for berries in hat using 6 strands of DMC #221 *Bumbleberry Red* floss.

Following General Instructions, sew inside border strips to wall hanging, trimming as needed. Repeat process for outside border.

Layer, quilt, and bind using your favorite method.

Using photograph as a guide, sew bee-shaped clay buttons to beekeeper and beehive appliqué blocks. If desired, apply powder blush with cotton swab to make cheeks on beekeeper.

Bee ye humble,
Bee ye kind,
Bee ye loving all the
time.

Bumblebee Wall Hanging

Approximate size: 18" x 23½"

SUPPLIES

Fat quarters, 2 from yellow prints, 2 from pastel prints, and 1 in muslin, for background blocks

Fat quarters or fabric scraps in assorted solids and prints for appliqué pieces:

  4 contrasting gold prints or solids for the beehives

  1 flesh for hands and face

  2 browns for the dog and shoes

  3 peach prints for flowers at the bottom and the heart in the hand

  2 cranberry or burgundy prints for the berries

  2 purple prints for small fowers

  1 yellow print for the center of flowers

  1 green print for the leaves

  3 coordinating/contrasting prints for the dress, apron, and hat

  1 print for the book

⅛ yard of contrasting print for inside border

½ yard of contrasting print for outside border and binding

Fat quarter of fabric for backing

DMC floss: #221 *Bumbleberry Red*, #310 *Charcoal Black*, #543 *Flax*, #801 *Dark Oak Brown*, #3740 *Plum*

Embroidery hoop and needle

Powder blush and cotton swab

5 bee-shaped clay buttons

½" round clay button

CUTTING

Cut a 9" x 11½" background block for girl appliqué.

Cut a 5½" x 6" background block for beehive appliqué.

Cut a 5½" x 6" background block for hand appliqué.

Cut a 14" x 5" muslin block for embroidered verse.

Cut a 14" x 4" background block for flower appliqué.

Cut two 1" x 20" strips for sides and two 1" x 15" strips for top and bottom of inside border.

Cut two 2½" x 19½" strips for sides and two 2½" x 18" strips for top and bottom of outside border.

Cut a 21" x 25" piece of fabric for backing.

ASSEMBLY

Enlarge patterns 135 percent and verse 200 percent.

Sew background blocks for beehive and hand appliqués together on one 5½" edge, as shown in Figure A.

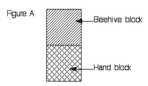

As shown in Figure B, sew background block for girl appliqué to Figure A unit.

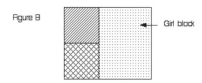

Transfer lettering for verse to appropriate backgound block and backstitch using 3 strands of DMC #221 *Bumbleberry Red* floss for larger words and 2 strands of the same floss for smaller words. Sew embroidered verse block to top of background block for flower appliqué.

As shown in Figure C, sew top of embroidered verse block to bottom of unit formed in Figure B.

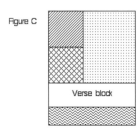

Using your favorite appliqué method, fuse or handstitch appliqué designs to corresponding background blocks according to pattern illustration.

Backstitch vines on beehive and beekeeper appliqués using 1 strand of DMC #801 *Dark Oak Brown* floss.

Make French knots for berries on beehive and girl appliqués using 3 strands of DMC #221 *Bumbleberry Red* floss.

Vine stitch girl's crook using 2 strands of DMC #3740 *Plum* floss.

Backstitch lines for girl's hair, dog's paws, and fur using 2 strands of DMC #801 *Dark Oak Brown* floss.

Using 2 strands of DMC #310 *Charcoal Black* floss,

backstitch lines for girl's shoelaces; make French knots for eyes using same thread.

Backstitch girl's thumb using 2 strands of DMC #543 *Flax* floss.

Following General Instructions, sew inside borders to wall hanging, trimming as needed. Repeat process for outside border.

If desired, apply powder blush with cotton swab to make cheeks on girl. Layer, quilt, and bind using your favorite method. Using the photograph of the wall hanging as a guide, sew bee-shaped clay buttons to flower and beekeeper appliqué blocks.

Sew a ½" round clay button on hand and heart appliqué.

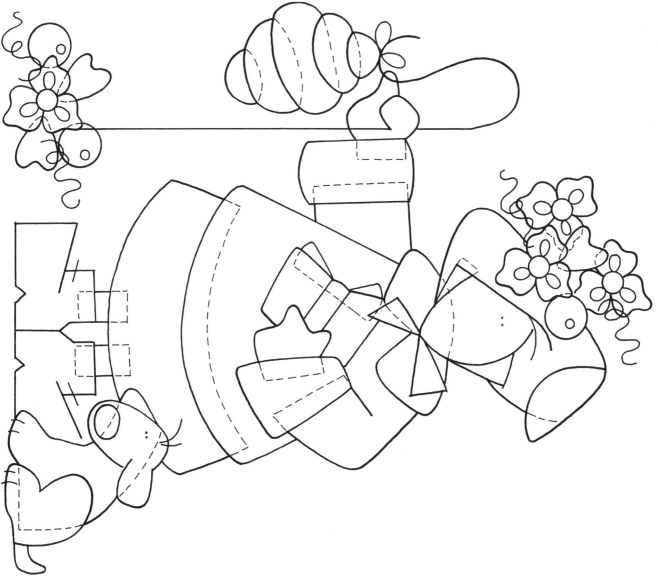

I'm bringing home a baby bumble bee.
Won't my mommy be so proud of me?
I'm bringing home a baby bumble bee.
Ouch! He stung me.

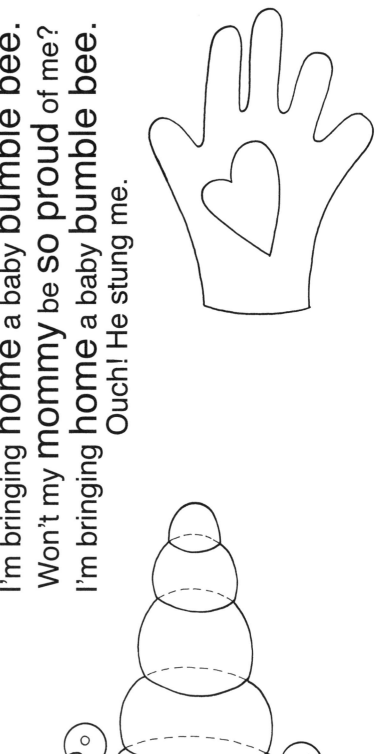

Beehive Topper Quilt

Approximate size: 47" x 47"

SUPPLIES

2⅔ yards of pale yellow or muslin fabric for background

1½ yards of contrasting print for outside quilt borders and binding

16 fat quarters or fabric scraps of different pastel prints for quilt blocks

3 yards of fabric for quilt back

DMC floss: #743 *Chamois Gold,* #833 *Pea Green,* #3779 *Pearl Pink,* #3041 *Wine Berry,* #801 *Dark Oak Brown,* #3042 *Lilac Heather*

Embroidery hoop and needle

ASSEMBLY

Use patterns at 100 percent.

Cut eight 10" squares of pale yellow or muslin fabric. Turn blocks on the point and transfer beehive design to center of each block.

Using 3 strands of floss, backstitch the beehive in DMC #743 *Chamois Gold,* leaves in DMC #833 *Pea Green,* berries in DMC #3779 *Pearl Pink,* and flowers in DMC #3041 *Wine Berry.*

Make a lazy daisy stitch in the center of each petal using DMC #743 *Chamois Gold* floss.

Outline center of flower with a backstitch using DMC #743 *Chamois Gold* floss, then fill flower centers with double-wrapped French knot clusters in DMC #3042 *Lilac Heather* floss.

With one strand of DMC #801 *Dark Oak Brown* floss, backstitch vines.

Press each embroidered block lightly on wrong side of fabric, being careful not to crush French knots.

Cut one hundred eight 2" squares from assorted pastel fabrics. Construct 12 nine-patch blocks as shown in Figure A, using colors randomly.

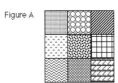

Figure A

Cut sixteen 5" x 2" strips of pale yellow or muslin fabric and sew to opposite sides of 8 of the nine-patch blocks, as shown in Figure B.

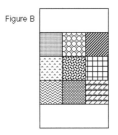

Figure B

Cut two 8" x 2" strips of pale yellow or muslin fabric and sew to the remaining sides of the 8 nine-patch blocks, as shown in Figure C. (Four of the nine-patch blocks will be used later for border treatment.)

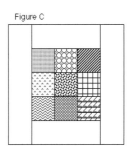

Figure C

From assorted pastel fabrics, cut 32 1½" squares and 32 strips measuring 8" x 1½" each. Sew strips to 2 opposite sides of the 8 bordered nine-patch squares, as shown in Figure D.

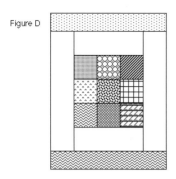
Figure D

Sew a 1½" square to each end of the 16 remaining 8" x 1½" strips, as shown in Figure E.

Figure E

Sew strips to opposite sides of the 8 nine-patch squares to complete the new border, as shown in Figure F.

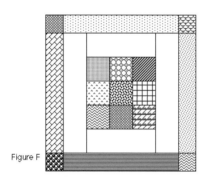
Figure F

From the assorted pastel fabrics, cut 8 honeybee pieces out of 1 print to make wings; cut 4 honeybee pieces out of a contrasting print to make bodies. Fuse or appliqué honeybee pieces to the pale yellow or muslin borders, as shown on sample. Repeat process using different print combinations for each of the 8 bordered nine-patch blocks.

Sew the beehive embroidered blocks and the 8 nine-patch honeybee blocks together, as shown in Figure G. Make sure all beehive blocks are facing the same direction.

☐ Embroidered block

▨ Nine-patch block

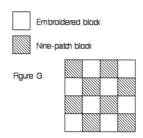
Figure G

Cut four 38½" x 2" strips of pale yellow or muslin background fabric and eight 38½" x 2" strips of border print. Construct 4 sets of 38½" strips, as shown in Figure H, and sew a set to the top and bottom of the quilt top.

Figure H
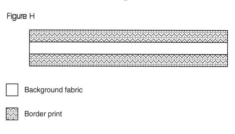

☐ Background fabric

▨ Border print

Sew the 4 reserved nine-patch blocks to the ends of the 2 remaining sets of 38½" strips, as shown in Figure I. Sew to the sides of the quilt top.

Figure I
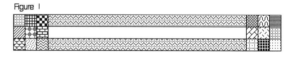

Cut a 52" square of fabric for backing. Layer, quilt, and bind using your favorite method.

Buzzing Blocks Quilt, Beyond the Garden Gate Quilt, "Bea in Her Bonnet" Doll with coat

Alphabet Sampler, "Bea in Her Bonnet" Doll with embroidered apron, *Beehive Pillow Topper, Buzzing Blocks Quilt*

Linen Tablecloth and Napkin Embroidery, Bumbleberry Embroidery

Beehive Topper Quilt, Busy as a Bee Pillow Embroidery, "Bea in Her Bonnet" Doll with Battenberg apron

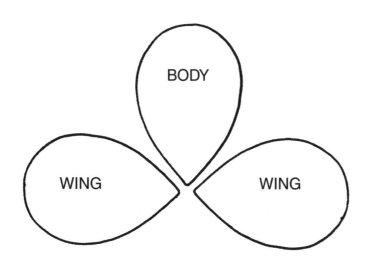

Beehive Pillow Topper

Approximate size: 46" x 62"

SUPPLIES

2 yards of print fabric for background

2¼ yards of pale yellow or muslin fabric for border

Fat quarters or scraps of the following:

  5 to 7 different gold prints for beehives

  2 cranberry or burgundy prints for berries

  2 dark green prints for leaves

  2 purple prints for 3-petal flowers

  2 peach prints for larger flowers

  1 yellow print or solid for flower centers

DMC floss: #801 *Dark Oak Brown*

Water erasable marker

Embroidery hoop and needle

4 bee-shaped clay buttons

2⅔ yards of fabric for backing

CUTTING

Cut two 56½" x 19" pieces from background fabric.

Cut three 56½" x 3½" strips from border fabric.

Cut two 3½" x 46½" strips from border fabric.

ASSEMBLY

First enlarge appliqué pattern 200 percent, then enlarge 175 percent.

Sew a 56½" border strip to the top and bottom of one background piece. Quick-fuse or appliqué designs to the bordered background piece, as shown on sample. Using a water erasable marker, trace embroidery lines onto the background fabric, overlapping appliqué pieces as shown on sample. Backstitch vines using 3 strands of DMC #801 *Dark Oak Brown* floss.

Sew remaining background piece to the top border of the appliquéd piece and add border strip to the top. Sew the 47" border strips to each side of the pillow topper, trimming as needed. Sew bee-shaped clay buttons to appliqué design as shown on sample. Layer, quilt, and bind using your favorite method.

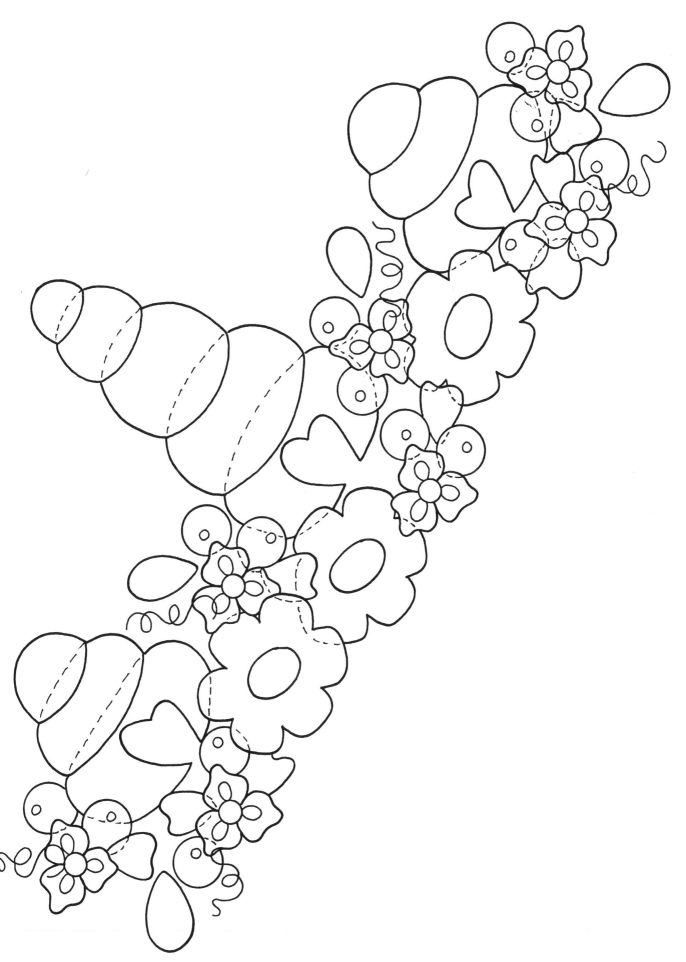

Buzzing Blocks Quilt

SUPPLIES

20 different pastel prints for quilt blocks*

1 yard of fabric for binding

Fabric for backing

    5 yards for twin

    6 yards for double

    8 yards for queen

    9 yards for king

CUTTING

Cut the number of 6½" squares as indicated for the size of quilt you wish to make:

    King (108" x 108"): 324 total blocks (approximately 17 blocks from each print)

    Queen (90" x 108"): 270 total blocks (approximately 14 blocks from each print)

    Double (84" x 96"): 224 total blocks (12 blocks from each print)

    Twin (72" x 90"): 180 total blocks (9 blocks from each print)

ASSEMBLY

Lay out blocks before sewing together to achieve desired color scheme arrangement. Sew blocks into rows as indicated for the size of quilt you are making:

King- and queen-size quilts require ⅝ yard of each fabric. Double- and twin-size quilts require ½ yard of each fabric.

King: 18 blocks per row, 18 rows in the quilt top

Queen: 15 blocks per row, 18 rows in the quilt top

Double: 14 blocks per row, 16 rows in the quilt top

Twin: 12 blocks per row, 15 rows in the quilt top

Hint: Add interest to the quilt by substituting some four-patch blocks in the design. To make a four-patch block, cut four 3½" squares and sew together.

Cut backing fabric approximately 2" larger than quilt top. Layer, quilt, and bind using your favorite method.

Option: Use borders on the back of the quilt to add interest when the quilt is reversed. Cut border strips 2½" wide to the desired length. Make a nine-patch block (see instructions for nine-patch blocks in Beehive Topper Quilt pattern) for the corners of the borders. Use your imagination to make your quilt back fun and interesting.

Busy as a Bee Pillow Embroidery

Approximate size: 15" round

SUPPLIES

½ yard of light-colored print or muslin fabric for background and backing of pillow

DMC floss: #743 *Chamois Gold*, #3041 *Wine Berry*, #3779 *Pearl Pink*, #833 *Pea Green*, #801 *Dark Oak Brown*, #3042 *Lilac Heather*

Water erasable marker

Polyfill for stuffing

Embroidery hoop and needle

ASSEMBLY

Enlarge pattern 200 percent.

Trace design onto background fabric using a water erasable marker. Unless otherwise indicated embroider design using a backstitch and 6 strands of DMC floss, in the following colors:

#743 *Chamois Gold*	beehive and outline for flower centers
#833 *Pea Green*	leaves
#3779 *Pearl Pink*	berry outline and centers
#3041 *Wine Berry*	flowers outline

Using DMC #3041 *Wine Berry* floss, make a lazy daisy stitch in the inside of each flower petal. Fill flower centers with double-wrapped French knots in DMC #3042 *Lilac Heather* floss.

Backstitch vines using 3 strands of DMC #801 *Dark Oak Brown* floss. Press lightly on wrong side of fabric to avoid crushing French knots.

Cut embroidered background fabric in a 16" circle, centering design. Cut another 16" circle for back of pillow. With right sides together, sew the two circles together, leaving a 4" opening at bottom. Clip curves, turn right side out, and stuff with polyfil. Close opening using a slip stitch. As an option, making a piping edge around the pillow in a contrasting print fabric.

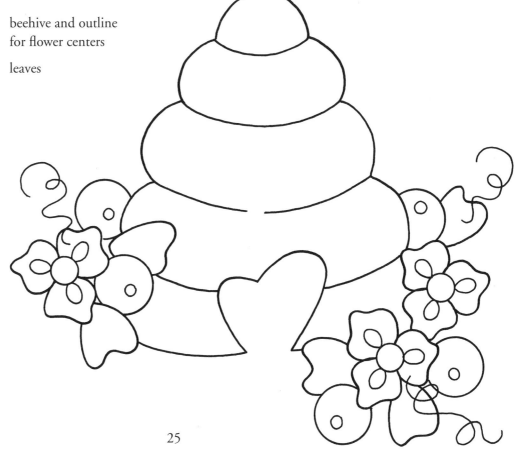

Bumbleberry Embroidery

Approximate size: 10½" x 13½" without matting or frame

SUPPLIES

⅝ yard of tea-dyed muslin, Ecology Cloth (or other high-thread count muslin), or osnaberg fabric

Water erasable marker

DMC floss: #221 *Bumbleberry Red*, #734 *Vintage Green*, #782 *Hazelnut*, #838 *Bark Brown*, #3011 *Dark Olive*, #3042 *Lilac Heather*, #3740 *Plum*, #3778 *Sachet Pink*

Embroidery hoop and needle

ASSEMBLY

Enlarge pattern 125 percent.

Cut a 20" x 30" piece of fabric and trace pattern onto fabric with a water erasable marker.

Unless otherwise indicated, embroider design using a backstitch and 3 strands of DMC floss in the following colors:

#782 *Hazelnut*	beehives
#3011 *Dark Olive* and #734 *Vintage Green*	leaves
#221 *Bumbleberry Red*	large berries
#3470 *Plum* and #3042 *Lilac Heather*	flowers
#782 *Hazelnut*	flower outline

Make a lazy daisy stitch in the center of each flower petal with a thread that matches petals. Fill centers with double-wrapped French knots using 3 strands of DMC #782 *Hazelnut* floss.

Create small berries with double-wrapped French knots using 3 strands of DMC #3778 *Sachet Pink* floss.

Backstitch vines using 1 strand of DMC #838 *Bark Brown* floss.

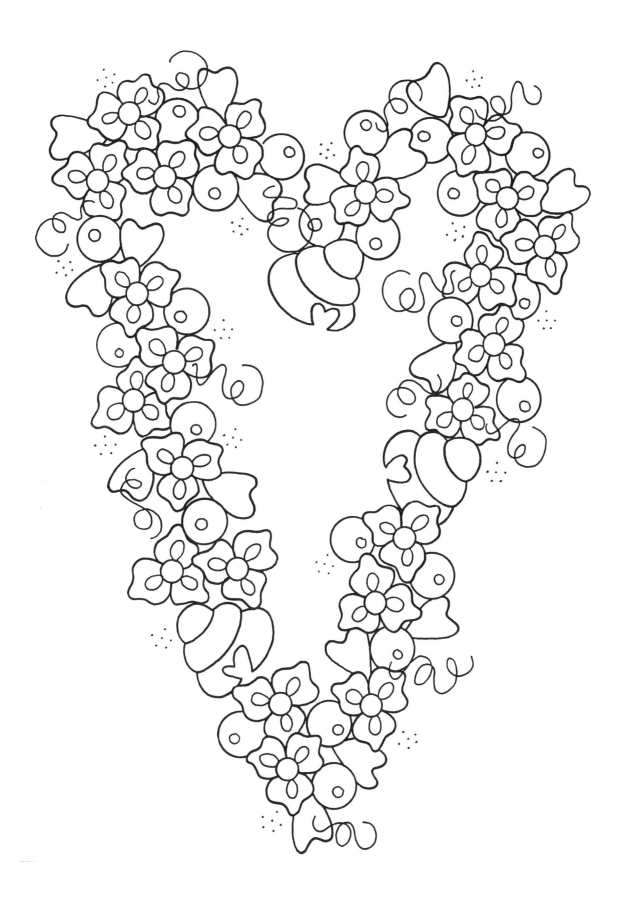

Alphabet Sampler

Approximate finished size: 8" x 22" without matting or frame

SUPPLIES

⅝ yard of tea-dyed muslin, Ecology Cloth (or other high-thread count muslin), or osnaberg fabric

Water erasable marker

DMC floss: #221 *Bumbleberry Red,* #310 *Charcoal Black,* #734 *Vintage Green,* #782 *Hazelnut,* #838 *Bark Brown,* #924 *Dark Aquamarine,* #926 *Aquamarine,* #927 *Pale Aquamarine,* #3011 *Dark Olive,* #3042 *Lilac Heather,* #3740 *Plum,* #3778 *Sachet Pink*

Embroidery hoop and needle

ASSEMBLY

Enlarge pattern 200 percent.

Cut a 16" x 30" piece of fabric and trace design onto fabric using a water erasable marker.

Using 3 strands of DMC floss, backstitch the following letters in the color indicated:

#924 *Dark Aquamarine:* Letters A, B, J, L, M, N, S, T, Y, and Z

#926 *Aquamarine:* Letters D, E, F, H, I, P, Q, R, and X

#927 *Pale Aquamarine:* Letters C, G, K, O, U, V, and W

Unless otherwise indicated, embroider design using a backstitch and 3 strands of DMC floss in the following colors:

#782 *Hazelnut*	beehives
#221 *Bumbleberry Red*	bumbleberries
#3470 *Plum* and #3042 *Lilac Heather*	flower outline and centers

Make a lazy daisy stitch in the center of each petal with a thread that matches flower petals. Fill centers with double-wrapped French knots in DMC #782 *Hazelnut* floss.

Create small berries with double-wrapped French knots in DMC #3778 *Sachet Pink* floss.

Vine stitch ruled lines in DMC #3740 *Plum* floss.

Using 2 strands of floss, backstitch leaves, alternating between DMC #3011 *Dark Olive* and #734 *Vintage Green.*

Backstitch verse using one strand of DMC #310 *Charcoal Black* floss.

a b c d e f
g h i j k l m

Bread and honey
are very nice.

Learn your alphabet
and get a slice.

n o p q r s
t u v w x y z

29

Linen Tablecloth and Napkin Embroidery

Approximate size: 52" square tablecloth, 18" napkin

SUPPLIES

52" square of premade cotton weave tablecloth (sample was made using a tablecloth from Wimpole Street)

18" square of premade cotton weave napkin (sample was made using a napkin from Wimpole Street)

DMC floss: #782 *Hazelnut*, #221 *Bumbleberry Red*, #3042 *Lilac Heather*, #3740 *Plum*, #3011 *Dark Olive*, #734 *Vintage Green*, #838 *Bark Brown*

Water erasable marker

Embroidery hoop and needle

ASSEMBLY

Tablecloth

Enlarge corner pattern 145 percent; use center piece at 100 percent.

With a water erasable marker, trace pattern onto tablecloth. You will need to flip the center pattern four times to obtain the circular design in the center of the tablecloth.

Unless otherwise indicated, embroider design using a backstitch and 6 strands of DMC floss in the following colors:

#782 *Hazelnut*	beehives
#221 *Bumbleberry Red*	bumbleberries
#3470 *Plum* and #3042 *Lilac Heather*	flower outline and centers
#3011 *Dark Olive* and #734 *Vintage Green*	leaves

Fill flower centers with single-wrapped French knots in DMC #782 *Hazelnut* floss. Backstitch vines using 3 strands of DMC #838 *Bark Brown* floss. Create small berries with single-wrapped French knots using 3 strands of DMC #782 *Hazelnut* floss.

Napkin

Use pattern at 100 percent. Center pattern in one corner and stitch embroidery design using same instructions as for tablecloth.

30

"Bea in Her Bonnet" Doll

SUPPLIES

1½ yards of tea-dyed muslin for body, legs, arms, and embroidered apron

1¼ yards of print fabric for dress

½ yard of coordinating fabric for pantaloons

½ yard of tea-dyed muslin or light-colored print for petticoat

1¼ yards of 2" wide lace for petticoat hem

⅓ yard of coordinating print fabric for legs

⅛ yard of white ribbing for stockings

2 precut squares of black felt for shoes

Leather soles (or additional precut black felt square) for shoes

Eight ¼" black clay buttons for shoes

2 yards of ⅜" wide lady chiffon ribbon for shoes (coordinate with dress color)

1 package Dizzie Frizzie®, Curly Tresses®, or mohair yarn for hair

#5 perle cotton to match body, pantaloons, and legs

#5 black perle cotton for shoes

Polyfil

3 cups poly pellets or filler beads

Embroidery needle and hoop

Water erasable marker

.05 ZIP permanent black ink pen

Powder blush and cotton swab

Additional Supplies for Optional Peter Pan Collar

¾" clay button

Additional Supplies for Optional Embroidered Battenberg Collar

8" round Battenberg doily

¾" clay button

Additional Supplies for Optional Battenberg Apron

15" x 21" white Battenberg tea towel

3" square white Battenberg doily

¼ yard of white cotton

Additional Supplies for Optional Embroidered Apron

2 fat quarters of print fabric to coordinate with dress

Nine ¼" clay buttons

Fat quarter of tea-dyed muslin

DMC floss: #221 *Bumbleberry Red*, #734 *Vintage Green*, #758 *Pink Grapefruit*, #783 *Golden Yellow*, #830 *Fatigue*, #838 *Bark Brown*, #3740 *Plum*, #3778 *Sachet Pink*

Additional Supplies for Optional Coat

½ yard of chenille to coordinate with dress

½ yard coordinating fabric for coat trim

Three 1" buttons

Additional Supplies for Optional Hat

¼ yard of coordinating print fabric to match dress

1 square precut white felt

1 yard of 1½" wide lady chiffon ribbon for hat ties

1 yard of 1½" wide spun-sugar ribbon for hat bow

Dried florals and greenery as desired

CUTTING (FOR PIECES WITHOUT PATTERNS)

From dress fabric cut two 3" x 5" pieces for cuffs, two 14" x 15" pieces for sleeves, and two 19" x 21" pieces for skirt.

From petticoat fabric cut one 18" x 21" piece.

From fabric for legs cut two 4½" x 18" strips.

From white ribbing cut two 6" x 4" pieces.

For optional coat cut two 4" x 11" cuffs from trim fabric.

For optional Battenberg apron, cut a 7" x 3" piece for waistband, two 3" x 21" strips for ties, and a 1½" x 8" strip for neckband from white cotton fabric.

For optional embroidered apron, cut fat quarters of two coordinating prints and tea-dyed muslin as follows:

Fabric A: Cut one 11½" x 19" piece for apron front
           Cut two 3" x 36" strips for apron ties
           Cut one 7" x 3" piece for waistband

Fabric B: Cut one 3½" x 19" strip for bottom of apron front

Muslin: Cut one 5" x 19" piece for embroidered section of apron front

ASSEMBLY OF BODY

Using patterns provided, trace and cut one body on fold and four arms out of tea-dyed muslin. Using a ¼" seam, sew a seam around entire body and miter bottom corners. Sew a seam around arms, leaving top open. Clip seams and turn arms right side out. Clip a 3" vertical opening in center back of body and turn body right side out. Fill body with 3 cups filler beads or poly pellets, then stuff firmly with Polyfil. Use perle cotton or thread and a whipstitch to close the opening. Stuff arms to within 2" of top and stitch to shoulder area of body.

Using the same fabric from which the leg pieces were cut, cut two foot pieces on the fold, as indicated on pattern. Unfold the fabric and sew each foot to a leg piece on the 4½" side with right sides together. Fold joined leg and foot piece lengthwise with right sides together; sew around the bottom of the foot to the top of the leg, leaving top open. Clip seams, turn right side out, and stuff to within 5" of top of leg.

Create "tube" socks by sewing the ribbing material along 6" side. Turn right side out and press top and bottom of socks under approximately ⅜". Slip sock onto leg and slide to top of foot, hiding seam. Repeat process for other leg. Using perle cotton or thread, whipstitch legs to body, with toes pointing inward.

ASSEMBLY OF CLOTHES

Dress

Trace and cut out bodice pattern on fold of dress fabric. Clip an opening for the neck, as indicated on pattern.

Gather sleeve pieces on 14" side and pull threads until sleeve fits on bodice. With right sides together, sew sleeves to bodice.

Fold cuff pieces in half along 3" side, with wrong sides together. This will create a 1½" x 5" band. Press cuffs.

Gather bottom edge of sleeves and pull threads until sleeve fits 5" raw edge of cuff piece.

With right sides together, sew sleeves to cuffs.

Gather skirt pieces along 19" side and pull threads until skirt pieces fit bodice. With right sides together, sew skirt pieces to bodice.

Starting at cuff, and keeping right sides together, sew up sleeve and down skirt. Repeat on other side of dress.

Using a rolled hem, turn dress skirt under and stitch a ½" hem.

Turn dress right side out and press lightly.

Carefully slip dress onto body and arms into sleeves. Cuffs will be snug to the arm and will need to be eased onto arms gently.

Dress Collar

To make a Peter Pan collar, cut two pieces from dress fabric on fold. With right sides together, stitch around the two collar pieces, leaving a 1" opening on inside back, as indicated on pattern. Clip seams and turn right side out. Turn raw edges of opening inside and press. Use a whipstitch to close the opening. Place collar around doll's neck and tack with thread at center back and each side of collar front. Sew a ¾" clay button to dress at center of collar.

For a Battenberg collar, trace embroidery pattern onto one side of a doily front, using a water erasable marker. With 3 strands of floss, backstitch flower using DMC #3778 *Sachet Pink* floss. With the same thread, make a lazy daisy stitch in the center of each flower. Backstitch leaf using 3 strands of DMC #734 *Vintage Green* floss. Backstitch vine using 1 strand of DMC #838 *Bark Brown* floss. Sew a ¾" clay button to center of the embroidered flower. Cut a 2" slit in center of doily, turn under raw edges and slip carefully over doll's head.

Collar may be omitted for optional coat variation.

Pantaloons

Trace and cut two pattern pieces on fabric fold, as indicated. With right sides together, sew crotch seam on both sides. Then rotate and match up legs and crotch seams. Sew from bottom of one pant leg up, across crotch seam, and down other leg. Turn right side out, fold under waist approximately ⅝" and press. Slip pantaloons onto body. With perle cotton and a large needle, use a running stitch to gather pantaloons at the waist and cinch up on the body. Tie and clip perle cotton. Turn pantaloons under 1" on bottom and hand gather with perle cotton ½" from bottom of pantaloons. Cinch firmly around each leg and tie off.

Petticoat

Sew lace to one 18" side of each petticoat piece with right sides together. Press seams. With right sides together, join the two 21" sides, forming one seam for the back and starting seam from the bottom (lace) edge. Turn right side out and press. Turn top of petticoat under 2" and press. With perle cotton, use a running stitch to hand gather waist 1" from top. Slip petticoat onto body, cinch firmly around waist, and tie off.

Battenberg Apron

Cut 2" off top of tea towel.

Fold waistband piece in half lengthwise and press.

Gather cut edge of tea towel and pull threads to fit waistband piece.

With right sides together, sew gathered tea towel to one thickness of the waistband.

Turn under remaining edge of waistband ¼" and whipstitch to wrong side of gathered tea towel. Press.

To create apron bib, align one edge of right side of doily with wrong side of apron along bottom edge of waistband and baste. Topstitch along top edge of waistband, securing doily in place. See diagram.

Press neckband piece in half lengthwise. Turn raw edges under ¼" and press. Use a topstitch along the open edge to close.

Sew each end of neckband to underneath side of doily at the top corner.

With right sides together, sew each apron tie along one short end and the long edge, leaving one short end open. Turn right side out and press.

Sew open end of apron ties to waistband. Slip neckband over body and tie apron around waist.

Embroidered Apron

Sew 11½" x 19" apron front piece to tea-dyed muslin along 19" side. Sew opposite edge of muslin piece to the 3½" x 19" piece of coordinating fabric. Press seams away from muslin section.

Trace embroidery pattern onto center of muslin piece. Using 3 strands of floss, backstitch leaves with DMC #830 *Fatigue* and #734 *Vintage Green,* alternating colors (refer to sample).

Backstitch berries using 3 strands of DMC #221 *Bumbleberry Red* floss. Backstitch beehive using 3 strands of DMC #783 *Golden Yellow* floss. Make French knots using 2 strands of DMC #3740 *Plum* floss. Backstitch vines using 1 strand of DMC #838 *Bark Brown* floss. Using 3 strands of floss, backstitch flowers with #758 *Pink Grapefruit* and #3778 *Sachet Pink,* alternately. Make a lazy daisy stitch in center of each petal with matching thread. Sew the 9 clay buttons to the center of each daisy.

Using a rolled hem, turn sides of apron under ½" and hem. Hem apron bottom under ¼". Fold and press waistband piece in half lengthwise.

Gather apron front at waist and pull threads to fit waistband. With right sides together, sew gathered apron front to one thickness of waistband. Turn under remaining edge of waistband ¼" and whipstitch to wrong side of gathered apron front. Press.

With right sides together, sew each apron tie along one short end and the long edge, leaving one short end open. Turn right side out and press. Sew open end of apron ties to waistband.)

Shoes

Trace and cut shoe patterns from black felt. Shoe sole may be made from either leather or felt. Stitch shoe tongue along straight line to inside center of upper shoe as indicated on pattern.

With right sides together, sew heel seam of upper shoe. Turn right side out and press seam open.

Sew shoe cuff to upper shoe as indicated on pattern. (Shoe cuff will be sewn to inside of upper shoe and folded over so cuff is on outside of shoe.)

Fold cuff down over shoe.

Using a blanket stitch, handstitch sole to upper shoe with black perle cotton. Sew 4 clay buttons on shoe, 2 on each side, as indicated on pattern.

Center length of ribbon around bottom buttons and criss-cross ribbon up and around top buttons. Put shoes on doll and tie ribbons in bow. You may need to use Polyfil to stuff toes of shoes.

Coat

Trace and cut coat pattern on two folds of chenille, as indicated on pattern.

Cut one coat collar piece from chenille on fabric fold, as indicated. Cut one coat collar piece from trim fabric. Cut 2" strips of trim fabric on the bias. Sew bias strips together to make approximately a 70" length of bias. Press one side of length under ¼."

Cut coat across top fold, as indicated on pattern, to make opening for neck.

Cut coat up front fold *only* and cut front corners as indicated on the pattern.

With wrong sides together, fold the cuffs in half length-wise. Sew the raw edge of the cuffs to the wrong side of the sleeve. Repeat for other sleeve. With right sides together, and starting from the bottom of the coat, sew up the side seams and down the arm, but *not across the cuff*. Clip seams. Turn right sides out. Sew across the cuff and fold it up over coat sleeve.

With right sides together, sew the bias strip from one side of the neck all the way around the coat. Allow for the bias to extend ½" beyond the neck on both sides. Fold the bias strip under ¼". Press, then fold in half and whipstitch to the wrong side of the coat.

With right sides together, sew chenille and trim collar pieces together, leaving a 1½" opening on inside neck back, as indicated on pattern. Clip seams and turn right side out. Stitch opening of collar closed. Tack collar onto neck of coat. Slip coat onto body.

Sew two buttons on left side of coat front. (Refer to sample for positioning.) Sew a third button at center of collar.

Hair

To make hair as seen in sample of doll with coat, use Dizzie Frizzie® yarn. Loop yarn around a 5" piece of cardboard 7 times. Remove from cardboard. Tie in center with matching yarn. Repeat ten times. Use hot glue or a needle and thread to attach hair sections to head.

For hair as shown on the doll with a Battenburg apron, use Curly Tresses® yarn. Loop yarn around 2" piece of cardboard seven times to make bangs. Stitch to center of head with a large needle and matching yarn. Loop yarn around 36" piece of cardboard or cutting board 30 times. Find center and stitch to center top of head. Tack sides of hair to neck with needle and yarn and tie firmly. Clip loops on either side and divide into thirds and braid hair to desired length. Loop braids up to neck and secure with a piece of matching yarn. Trim any excess and tie with ribbon at top of loops.

To make hair as shown in the sample doll with an embroidered apron, use mohair yarn. To make bangs, loop yarn around a 2" piece of cardboard seven times. Stitch bangs to center of head with a large needle and matching yarn. Loop yarn around a 24" quilters rule 30 times. Center loops on top of head and stitch down with large needle and a piece of matching yarn. Clip bottom of loops and trim hair length evenly.

Hat

Trace and cut out two hat pieces from the provided pattern. *Do not cut out center yet.*

Using the same pattern, cut out one hat piece from white felt. *Do not cut out center yet.*

Layer the pieces with the right sides of the print fabric together and the felt pieces underneath the fabric. Sew a ¼" seam around outside only. Clip seams.

Trace center opening from pattern onto felt piece using a pencil or a water erasable marker.

Cut out center piece, going through all three thicknesses. Turn right side out and press. (Felt piece will now be between the fabric pieces.)

For decorative purposes only, topstitch around outside of hat ¼" from edge, then topstitch again ¼" from the first topstitching.

Topstitch ¼" from raw edge around center opening.

Cut two 18" lengths of ribbon for hat ties and tack to underneath side of the hat, where hair will hide. Place hat on head and hot glue several dried or silk florals and greenery of your choice to cover center opening of hat. Bows made from additional lengths of ribbon may also be used.

Finishing Touches

Using a ZIG pen, draw on eyes, eyelashes, and freckles. Use powder blush and cotton swab to blush checks.

Enlarge shoe tounge and foot 135 percent

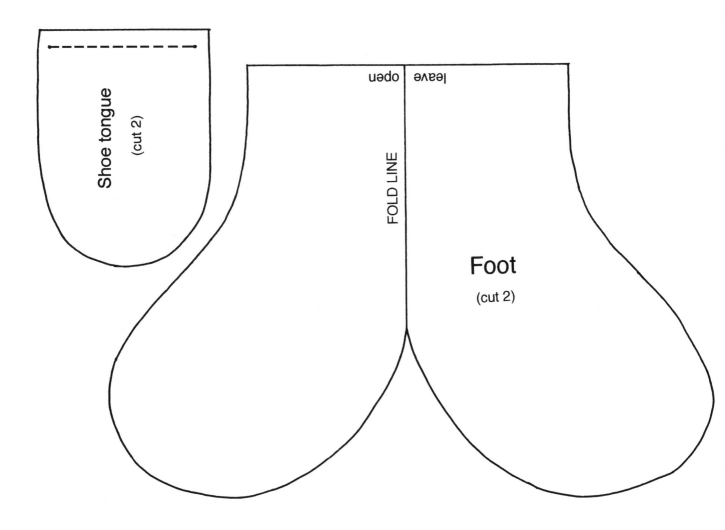

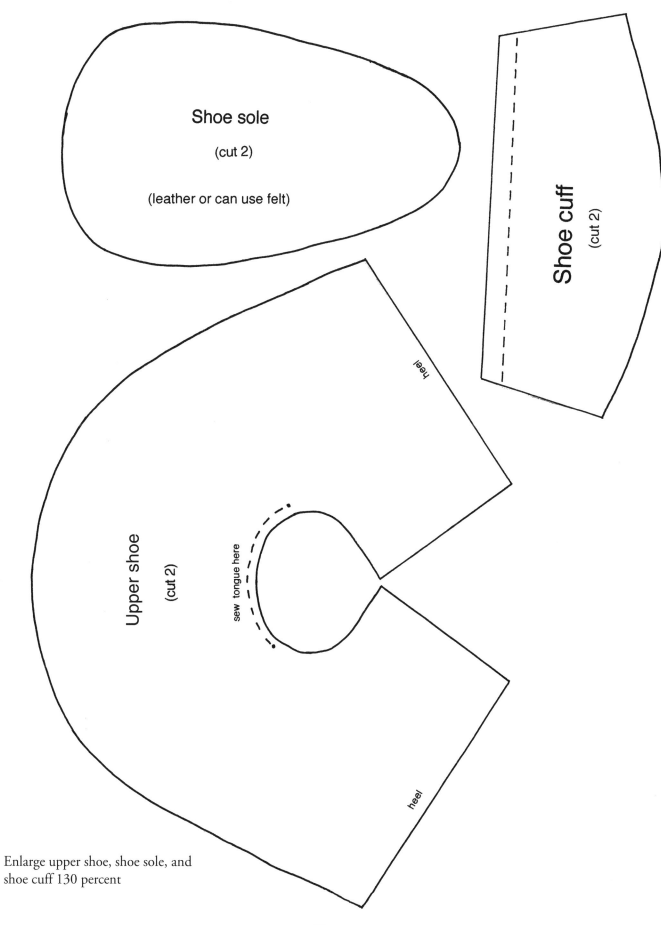

Shoe sole

(cut 2)

(leather or can use felt)

Shoe cuff

(cut 2)

Upper shoe

(cut 2)

sew tongue here

heel

heel

Enlarge upper shoe, shoe sole, and
shoe cuff 130 percent

Enlarge coat collar and dress bodice 132 percent

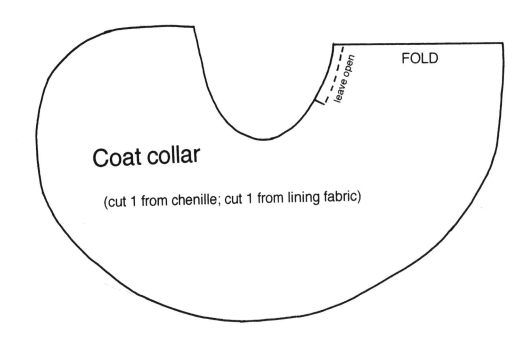

Coat collar

(cut 1 from chenille; cut 1 from lining fabric)

FOLD

leave open

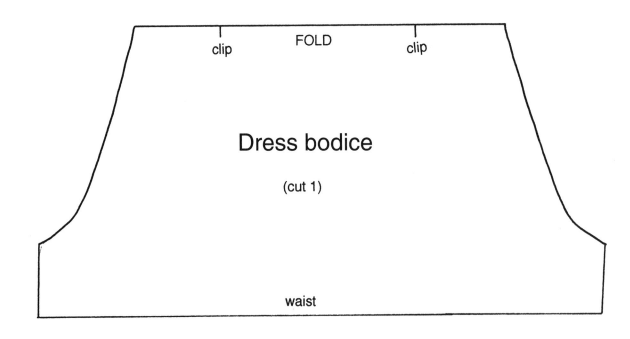

clip   FOLD   clip

Dress bodice

(cut 1)

waist

Enlarge coat 200 percent

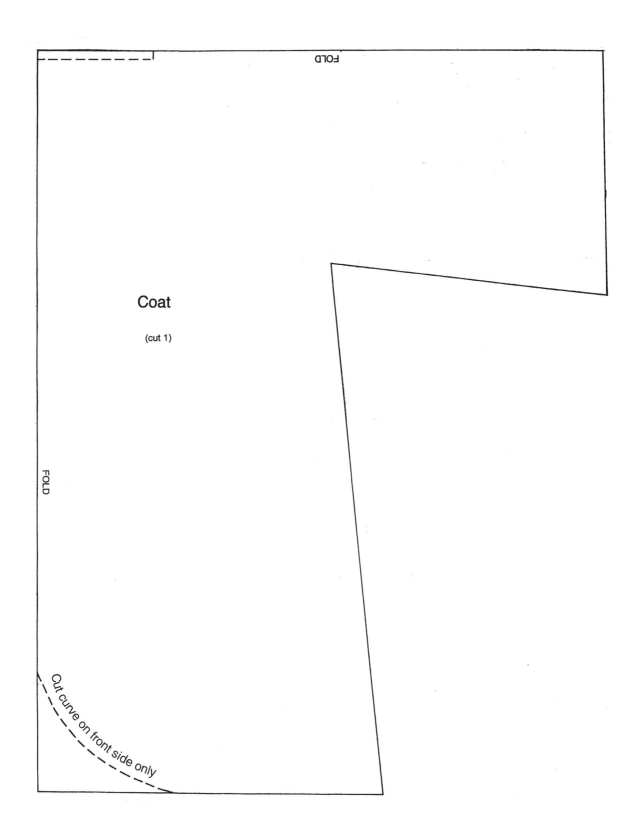

Coat

(cut 1)

FOLD

FOLD

Cut curve on front side only

Enlarge pantaloons 200 percent

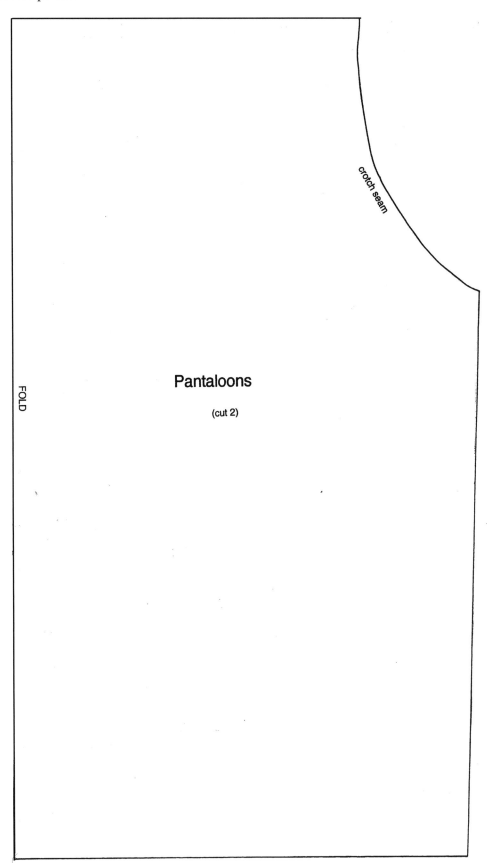

Pantaloons

(cut 2)

FOLD

crotch seam

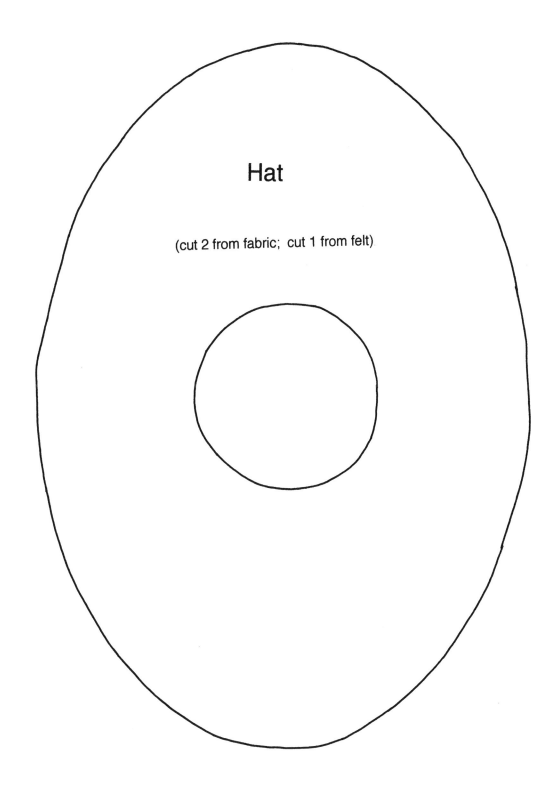

Hat

(cut 2 from fabric; cut 1 from felt)

Enlarge arm and body 200 percent

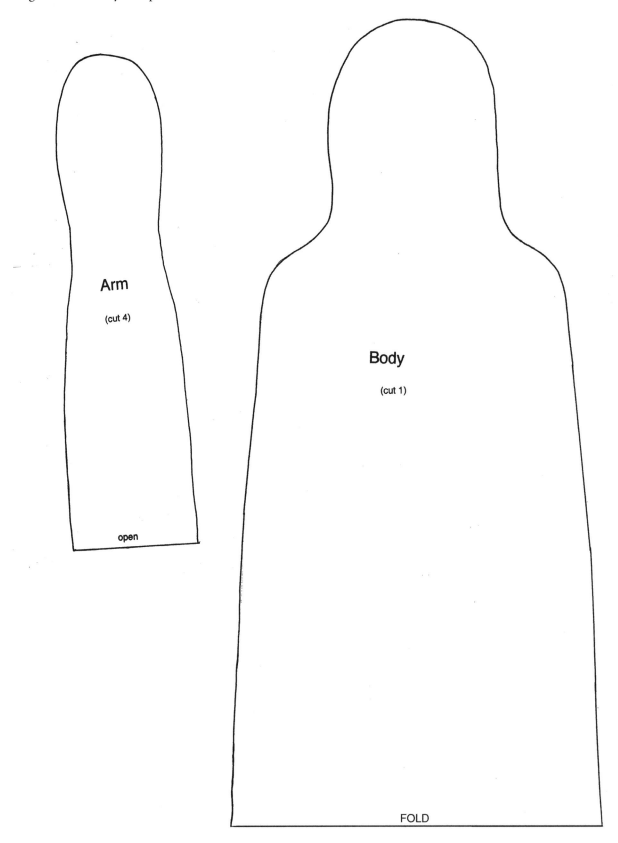

Arm

(cut 4)

open

Body

(cut 1)

FOLD

Embroidery for doll apron and collar

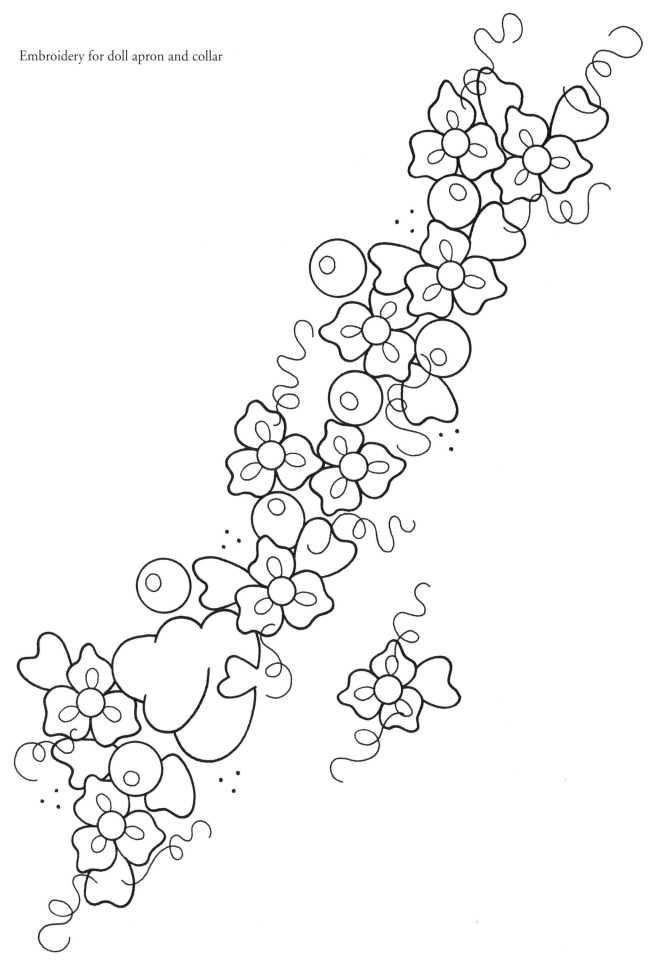